THE EIGHT (8) GUIDELINES FOR A SUCCESSFUL MARRIAGE

By; Wanda B. Roberts

Table of contents

Introduction

There is no manual for life's most challenging tasks, especially marriage, which has its ups and downs. These guidelines have been developed through several years of couple-focused longitudinal research. Although it takes time to apply these ideas, doing so can be crucial to building a strong bond with your spouse.

Chapter 1

Improve your love maps

A lovemap is an idea started to help a conversation of why individuals like what they like sexuoerotically. It is "a formative portrayal or layout in the psyche and in the cerebrum portraying the glorified sweetheart and the romanticized program of sexuoerotic movement projected in symbolism or really participated in with that darling."

A lovemap can be formed by both positive and pessimistic elements, things that draw in or repulse the individual whose suggestive preferences are being planned. Because of reasons that are not generally straightforward, one individual might be drawn to individuals of a specific orientation, with a specific actual trademark, with specific character qualities, etc. One may likewise find specific attributes so undermining or questionable that it unequivocally mitigates against a sensual fascination being showed.

A lovemap can be molded by natural factors that work with the development of a sexual bond, or that upgrade or reduce suggestive reaction. For example, certain individuals might bond emphatically to individuals with whom they share an emergency circumstance. Certain individuals might find their sensual reactions quieted within the sight of threatening natural elements (attentive elderly folks or meddling neighbors, for example).

Anyway, how comfortable would you say you are with your companion's internal world? What do you are familiar your accomplice's set of experiences, concerns, inclinations, stresses, and the ongoing scene? How would you refresh your insight into your companion's inward world?

In over forty years of examination with more than 3000 couples, research observed that genuinely shrewd couples are personally acquainted with one another's reality. It's call having a lavishly point by point love map and its the term for that piece of the cerebrum where you store all the significant data about your accomplice's life. One more method for saying this is that they have set aside a lot of mental space for their marriage. They recall the significant occasions in one another's set of experiences, and they continue to refresh their data as current realities and sensations of their life partner's reality change.

Without such an affection map, you can't actually know your mate. Furthermore, on the off chance that you don't actually know somebody, how might you genuinely cherish them?

Such information likewise gives the strength to climate conjugal tempests. Couples who have definite love guides of one another's reality are much better ready to adapt to upsetting occasions and struggle. For instance, the introduction of the principal child is one of the significant reasons for conjugal disappointment and separation. 67% of couples in research went through a steep drop in conjugal fulfillment whenever they first became guardians. Be that as it may, the leftover 33% didn't encounter this decay, truth be told, about portion of them saw their marriage move along. Which isolated these two gatherings? The couples whose relationships flourished after the birth had definite love maps all along. These affection maps safeguarded their relationships right after this emotional disturbance.

All in all, how might you upgrade your affection maps? The cycle involves posing unassuming inquiries and afterward recalling the responses. An inquiry without a right or wrong answer is one that can't be replied with a speedy "yes" or "no." Instead, it welcomes your accomplice to propose their encounters, suppositions, and feelings. Posing an unconditional inquiry shows a real interest in your accomplice's live and inward world. "Did you call the handyman today?" isn't an inquiry that enlightens you much regarding your accomplice's interior world. Notwithstanding, questions like, "How might you like our life to change in the following 5 years?" and "Assuming you had all the cash on the planet, what might your fantasy house be like?" will uncover to you something else about your companion's internal world.

Getting to realize your companion better and imparting your internal identity to your accomplice is a continuous cycle. It's a deep rooted process, truth be told. "Sincerely insightful couples are know all about their accomplices' adoration maps." Improving your affection maps is tied in with being know about your accomplice's reality and figuring out their lived insight, knowing their way to express affection, and recalling their groundbreaking occasions. Common comprehension of one another's universes can excite care for one another and increment association.

Improving your adoration maps includes a profound perception of what makes your accomplice your accomplice. A few inquiries you might ponder or attempt to reply about your accomplice include:

- What are their best three main tunes and why?
- What is their greatest apprehension?
- What are a few dreams they have for what's to come?
- What worries them?
- What are a portion of the significant occasions that have happened in their life?

These model inquiries can provide you with a thought of how comfortable you are with your accomplice's affection map. Assuming you notice this is a region lacking, it doesn't be guaranteed to mean your marriage is ill-fated to fizzle. Upgrading your adoration map through fair conversation is conceivable.

Chapter 2

Sustain your affection and appreciation

We are know about the main phase of a relationship where you are "thoroughly blindly enamored" with your accomplice. You can't get enough of that person, you need to spend each waking (and dozing) minute together, all that he/she does is charming, and you have such a lot of deference for him/her. This underlying phase of fixation is described by serious affection and deference for your accomplice, however as any of us realize who have been seeing someone a little longer, that first stage begins to blur after around two years. "What we used to find charming can immediately turn into a propensity that truly disturbs us." as a matter of fact, this stage alone is logical an essential explanation regarding the reason why such countless individuals have searched out relationship marriage mentoring. This underlying stage is maintained and supported by heartfelt fascination and as it blurs several begins to see their relationship in a more sensible light. It is from this more sensible viewpoint that a fundamental reason for the relationship going into the future can be fabricated.

Saying this doesn't imply that that heartfelt fascination is definitely not a critical component of a personal connection nor that it is contradictory with building veritable deference and affection for your accomplice.

Affection and deference in marriage show liking for your accomplice, in light of an internal conviction that they deserve regard and I make sense of that the marriage may presently not be salvageable when affection and esteem are deficient. However, there's a decent approach to assessing whether you have esteem and affection for your marriage which is to tell the narrative of your most memorable gathering and romance. Research found that the manner in which couples tell their relationship beginnings story anticipated separate or conjugal soundness with a 94% precision.

Affection and esteem are critical to cheerful connections. Recalling your accomplice's positive characteristics reinforces the connection between you, even as you battle with one another's imperfections. A more grounded bond makes it simpler to resolve issues and execute arrangements. Affection and esteem are likewise counteractants to disdain.

Keeping a feeling of regard for your accomplice goes far in lessening the impacts of the Four Horsemen (scorn, analysis, preventiveness, and stalling) when you clash.

Sensations of affection and deference can be reinforced by showing appreciation and appreciation for your accomplice. They don't need to be amazing motions. All things being equal, center around the easily overlooked details your accomplice in all actuality does right over the course of the day. When you see your accomplice making a garbage run, do you tell them you're thankful for them? Following a bustling day, thank your accomplice for getting those things done you couldn't get to.

As straightforward as it might sound, cheerfully wedded couples like one another. Cheerful accomplices keep up with deference for one another in any event, during conflicts and help themselves to remember the positive characteristics about their accomplice. Despite the fact that enjoying your accomplice sounds simple, couples frequently wind up caught in sensations of scorn or even revulsion with regards to their accomplice. Eye rolls, jeers, and mockery are certain signs your sentiments may be going down a negative street. The cure? Sustaining your affection and adoration. It's not difficult to see the things your accomplice is fouling up, however it's similarly as simple to see the things your accomplice is doing well.

In the event that you are battling with sensations of affection and esteem for your accomplice, the following are several inquiries to ponder:

- What do I esteem about my accomplice?
- What positive characteristics does my accomplice have?
- In what ways might I at some point tell my accomplice I value them?
- Am I zeroing in on what my accomplice fouls up more frequently than on what my accomplice does well?
- How would I as of now told my accomplice I value them and our relationship?
- Am I demonstrating the conduct I anticipate from my accomplice?

Sustaining affection and reverence is a center device for producing energy in a relationship. In this way, find opportunity to create and communicate the good sentiments you have for your accomplice. Cause creating and communicating affection and esteem a piece of how you to cooperate with your accomplice on an everyday premise, and notice how it improves the caring kinship you are working with your accomplice.

Sustaining your relationship might seem to be this:

- ➢ Arranging date evenings together
- ➢ Attempting another side interest or movement together
- ➢ Communicating appreciation for your companion
- ➢ Commending your accomplice

On the off chance that supporting affection toward your life partner isn't really important, you might think about consulting a couples therapist.

Chapter 3

Quality time

Several requirements quality time together for the relationship to develop and to create. The fact that quality time centers around harmony. Everything revolves around communicating your adoration and love with your full focus.

At the point when you're with your accomplice, you put down the smartphones, switch off the tablet, and spotlight on them. Furthermore, when that's what you do, it contacts their heart in a way that truly matters. They feel significant, cherished, and exceptional like you were deliberate in carving out opportunity only for them. Sadly, because of innovation, quality time with our accomplices is turning out to be increasingly scant. In any event, when we are together, we are somewhere else as a rule in the Internet or somewhere down in our own contemplations. Yet, being in closeness to each other while accomplishing something different doesn't necessarily comprise quality time, regardless of how long you stay there. Also, for somebody whose essential way to express affection is quality time, this absence of connectedness can let them feeling unfilled and be.

❖The most effective method to Give Your Partner Quality Time

With regards to making quality time for your accomplice, you must do things that will cause your accomplice to feel adored and appreciated.

Coming up next are a portion of the manners in which you can show your quality time accomplice that you love them;

✓Visually engage

With regards to quality time, eye to eye connection is the doorway to adoring your quality time accomplice. Truth be told, keeping in touch lets your accomplice know that they certainly stand out enough to be noticed, which will cause them to feel cherished, significant, and comprehended. It additionally imparts that you care about what they need to say. Yet, when you are diverted and looking at your telephone while your accomplice discusses their day, they will feel like you simply couldn't care less about what they need to say and, likewise, that you couldn't care less about them.

✓ Utilize Active Listening Skills

Undivided attention is perhaps of the most cherishing thing you can accomplish for your accomplice, however for some individuals, this doesn't fall into place easily. All things considered, a great many people contemplate their own considerations and feelings more than they ponder their accomplice's.

At the point when quality time individuals are talking, attempt the accompanying undivided attention abilities:

- Center around what they are talking about.
- Incline in somewhat.
- Assert what they are talking about.
- Pose insightful inquiries.
- Try not to attempt to offer counsel, except if they request it.
- Have a go at imagining their perspective or contemplating how you could feel experiencing the same thing.

Quality time accomplices are more keen on feeling comprehended. They are searching for sympathy and empathy and don't necessarily need to have their circumstances fixed.

✓ Put down certain boundaries on Technology

Nothing harms a quality time individual more than to share something they feel is truly significant, and afterward to gaze upward and understand their accomplice is just half focusing while at the same time attempting to answer an email from a collaborator or answer a text. Practice it regularly to take care of your telephone at supper or during a short breather and truly center around what your accomplice needs to say. Despite the fact that you may not examine anything momentous, you are making a significant and cherishing motion by picking your accomplice over innovation.

✓ Center around Quality, Not Quantity

With regards to quality time, it's not necessary to focus on how much time you spend together yet rather the nature of your collaborations that count. What's more, with such a lot of happening in your life, cutting out a couple of moments for a significant and continuous discussion can be a superb method for showing the individual you love that you give it a second thought. The key is that you require some investment to appreciate each others conversation, regardless of whether it is simply sitting on the sofa partaking in some espresso before work. Keep in mind, it's really not necessary to focus on the amount of time you spend together, yet rather the quality.

✓ Foster a Routine

Search for little ways of interfacing with your accomplice consistently. For example, you could implore or contemplate together each day or perused the Sunday funnies together every week. Tracking down a little approach to consistently interface will assist your quality time with cooperating feel satisfied and appreciated. In addition, it's something you can both anticipate doing together.

✓ Be Present and Available

At the point when your accomplice is feeling unreliable or going through a difficult stretch, you can truly show you care by just being there and hanging out. Despite the fact that you will not have the option to remove all the distress nor would it be advisable for you be supposed to you will actually want to show that you are available and accessible when they need you.

✓ Remain at the Time

For individuals whose essential way to express affection is quality time, they never neglect to focus on the way that time is restricted and tomorrow isn't guaranteed. Therefore, they view time all together present that they need to give and get in connections. To them, life is tied in with being at the time more than it is about the thing you are doing. It's likewise about focusing on your loved ones over all the other things.

So with regards to quality time, a great many people expect it implies really getting to know each other or going out a ton. Assuming that were the situation, attempting to show your accomplice you care through quality time could get debilitating and costly.

Be that as it may, cherishing an accomplice who wants quality time really has next to no to do with how much time you are together. It's likewise not in light of exercises. Quality time is about how you invest the energy that you have together. Regardless of what you are doing, assuming that you are mindful and centered, your accomplice will feel cherished.

Chapter 4

Move in the direction of one another rather than away

This is a really mind blowing piece of information. It recommends that there is something you can do today that will emphatically redirect your relationship. All the more critically, it proposes that there is something that you can't do that will prompt its death. Anyway, how would you dismiss towards rather than? To comprehend turning, you need to initially grasp offers.

❖Turn towards what? Bids for association

A bid is any endeavor starting with one accomplice then onto the next for consideration, insistence, love, or some other positive association. Offers appear in basic ways, a grin or wink, and more complicated ways, similar to a solicitation for guidance or help. As a rule, ladies make a bigger number of offers than men, yet in the best connections, the two accomplices are open to making a wide range of offers. Offers can get precarious, notwithstanding, and honestly I here and there miss a bigger number of offers than I don't. To be sure numerous men battle in such manner, so focusing is significant. You really should figure out how to perceive offers and that you focus on making them to each other. Make "offers" part of your discussion and maybe name your offers toward each other. It's OK to say, "I'm making a bid for consideration now" as you get to know one another in this beginning stage of your relationship. You can likewise work on knowing subtext together. Pick a show that is different to you both and watch it on quiet. Check whether you can decipher the offers that the characters make dependent just upon non-verbals. When you begin to become deliberate about your offers, you can focus on "turning towards."

To "miss" a bid is to "dismiss." Turning away can obliterate. It's considerably more decimating than "betraying" or dismissing the bid. Dismissing a bid basically gives the valuable chance to proceeded with commitment and fix. Missing the bid brings about reduced offers, or more regrettable, making offers for consideration, happiness, and warmth elsewhere.

"Normal Mistakes to Avoid"

On occasion, it very well may be difficult to see a bid from your accomplice, particularly if both of you are not in great term. However, you will ultimately get its hang. The key is to keep away from a couple of these normal errors.

- Try not to whine about the offers your accomplice is making .
- Fight the temptation to accomplish something different while your accomplice is wanting for consideration.
- Try not to see your accomplice as destitute.
- Keep all that can dismiss you from your accomplice hidden away.
- Remember to ask what your accomplice needs to feel cherished.
- In a sound relationship, accomplices make offers for one another's consideration.

In the event that you tell your accomplice, "I'm having a terrible day at work," and your accomplice answers, "I lack opportunity and willpower to talk the present moment," this is getting some distance from one another. At the point when your accomplice offers for your consideration and you get some margin to be available, tune in, and support them, you're turning toward each other.

❖How to turn towards? Focus on your accomplice

Turning towards begins with focusing. Your work on offers will prove to be useful here. Basically perceiving that a bid was made makes the way for the reaction. In the event that you focus, you'll answer both the text and the subtext. As offers get more muddled, so will the idea of moving in the direction of. For the time being, begin straightforward. Take a stock of the offers and turning in your relationship and offer your reactions with each other.

- What do I am familiar with how I make offers?
- Could or would it be advisable for me to get better at making offers? How?
- How great am I at perceiving the distinction among text and subtext?
- What holds me back from making offers?
- What is my motivation for turning?
- Do I dismiss or against more frequently than I turn towards?
- With regards to turning towards, am I closer to 33% or 86%?
- What does it seem like when my accomplice doesn't turn towards me?
- How might I get better at turning towards?

"Moving in the direction of is the premise of close to home association, sentiment, enthusiasm, and a decent sexual coexistence." Choosing to move in the direction of one another aides fill one another's "adoration tank," Then, when times get hard, that full tank can prove to be useful and help you pass through the test gainfully and affectionately.

Chapter 5

Allow your accomplice to impact you

Couples are bound to remain together when they fill in collectively. At the point when one individual has all the power in a relationship, it makes a hierarchal contrast. At the point when you permit your accomplice to impact you while pursuing huge choices, imparting insights, or including your companion in your manner of thinking, you permit them to impact you.

Allowing your accomplice to impact you isn't equivalent to permitting another person to control you. It's more about conveying and including your better half in choices. Regardless of whether you deviate, there are still ways of having quiet, normal conversations that extend regard toward your soul mate.

In principle, the vast majority concur that it's really smart for the two accomplices in a relationship to have impact in navigation. You envision you're great at filling in collectively, splitting the difference, and going this way and that, if by some stroke of good luck your accomplice would be more adaptable. Research led showed that men who acknowledge impact from their female accomplices will quite often have more joyful and additional fantastic connections. Oddly, what the exploration likewise showed was that the more impact an accomplice was ready to acknowledge, the more compelling that accomplice was in the relationship by and large. In actuality, tolerating impact is an equivalent open door idea. All close connections work better when the two accomplices have and acknowledge impact. Truth be told, this is one of the signs of an effective relationship, one in which there is an example of conscious impact going this way and that and the two accomplices feel that things are fair.

❖What's the significance here to acknowledge impact?

In examining this thought in couples treatment, there's occasionally a conviction that you need to consent or simply oblige your accomplice to acknowledge impact really. "On the off chance that I simply say 'OK, dear,' all is well," a client shared with me as of late. This is a mixed up conviction, as tolerating impact is basically being available to the thoughts and assessments of your accomplice, not concurring or consenting or yielding. By tolerating impact, you recognize that your accomplice has a legitimate perspective. You invite it, will be affected, and perhaps have your point of view changed by it. According to tolerating impact, "You are significant, and your viewpoints make a difference to me regardless of whether (and extra focuses for this, particularly if) I disagree with you."

Issues with opposing impact appear in numerous ways. Some are obviously around one accomplice dismissing the other or expecting to constantly have their own specific manner. Others are more unpretentious, for example, one accomplice seeming to look for input on something when in the background they have gone with their choice as of now. Certain individuals reflexively say or designate "no" as a method for keeping up with command over a discussion or choice regardless of whether they really concur with their accomplice. There can be justifiable explanations behind any of these positions, however it's essential to take note of that the main message that is getting imparted to the accomplice is "No."

On the opposite finish of the range are individuals brought up in families or by social or cultural standards to accept that they don't have the right to have impact, so what is the point of shouting out? They think, 'It won't go anyplace.' Both closures of this range can make power battling and hatred.

❖The most effective method to acknowledge impact

All in all, how might you stay away from the pulls of-war that occur around this issue of impact?

To start with, really look at yourself. Mindfulness is critical. You're possible making an effort not to close your accomplice down yet are unintentionally doing as such. That can seem like, "I'm simply offering my viewpoint" when in actuality they're thinking '... and this is the main assessment that is important.' Ask yourself, would you say you are truly remaining open to the next point of view?

Tune in with interest to the next perspective. Verify whether you are seeing accurately. It is such a ton harder to do this when you dissent, yet the arrangement you can at last come to will feel improved if both of you feel comprehended and regarded. Recollect the examination. "The more impact you acknowledge, the more persuasive you will be."Search for ways of saying "OK." There is an advantage to you in yielding a little, not being protective, and being available to seeing that your accomplice has a legitimate point of view — regardless of whether you share it. Consider it searching for ways of saying "OK," regardless of whether that is a basic affirmation, for example, "I see your point." For some, this can be a test, yet you need to ask yourself: Do you need to be correct or would you like to remain together?

Chapter 6

Take care of your reasonable issues

There are two sorts of issues that can happen in a marriage: unending and feasible.

Never-ending issues normally are perplexing and may bring about correspondence gridlock. Yet, in light of the fact that you definitely disapprove of your life partner doesn't mean you can't have a flourishing marriage.

Resolvable issues are normally more clear. With resolvable issues, you can straightforwardly handle the issue and track down an answer. Be that as it may, on the grounds that an issue is feasible doesn't mean it will be effectively settled. In the event that you wind up battling to determine your struggles and you have recognized these contentions as feasible, then perhaps you want to adopt an alternate strategy to settling them.

On the off chance that you'll understand these means, I think you'll find you can take care of much a bigger number of issues and in a better manner than you have previously. After numerous long periods of examining and exploring how cheerful couples settled their contentions and found another model for settling struggle in a caring relationship. Cry are the moves toward follow:

- ❖Mellow your startup
- ❖Figure out how to make and get fix endeavors
- ❖Mitigate yourself and one another
- ❖Split the difference
- ❖Be lenient toward one another's deficiencies

These means will be more straightforward for some than for others in light of your childhood and how you approach relationships now, yet simple or hard, they will be compelling in the event that you can follow them.

❖Mellow Your Startup

In both cheerful and miserable relationships, the spouse is generally the one to raise a delicate issue and push to determine it. The large contrast between the two is the means by which the spouse brings it up. Starting a discussion with a basic/mocking remark or motion (unforgiving startup) essentially destines it to disappointment. A delicate startup, in any case, where you convey your solicitation with adoration, regard, and thought reassures your companion and cultivates a protected climate for conversation. Mellowing the startup is critical to settling clashes since research has shown that conversations constantly end on similar note they start.

Here are a few ideas to guarantee your startup is delicate:

- Grumble yet don't fault
- Offer expressions that beginning with "I" rather than "You"
- Portray what's going on, don't assess or pass judgment
- Be clear
- Be amenable
- Be grateful
- Try not to store things up

❖Figure out how to make and get fix endeavors

At the point when your conversation gets going all wrong, or you end up in an unending pattern of recriminations, you can forestall a fiasco on the off chance that you know how to stop. I call these brakes fix endeavors. Fix endeavors are endeavors several makes to deescalate the strain during a tricky conversation. At the point when I want to de-heighten a conversation with my better half, I frequently use humor

as my maintenance endeavor. It diffuses the pressure so we can get the conversation again in a more loosened up climate. There are innumerable ways of bringing fix endeavors into your conversations and they will be different for each couple. You want to find what works for you as a team.

Here is a concise testing of some maintenance endeavors you could utilize:

- I feel reprimanded, might you at any point reword that?
- Might we at any point have some time off?
- I truly blew that one
- How might I improve things?
- Please accept my apologies, if it's not too much trouble, pardon me
- I never considered things that way
- I see what you're referring to
- We are becoming derailed
- I'm feeling overwhelmed

- I see your point
- I'm grateful for...
- One thing I respect about you is...

❖Mitigate Yourself and One Another

In by far most of cases, when one companion doesn't "get" the other's maintenance endeavor, this is on the grounds that the audience is overwhelmed and hence can't sincerely hear what the mate is talking about. At the point when you're in this condition, the most smart fix endeavor on the planet won't help your marriage. Your heart might be beating, you're perspiring, you're pausing your breathing, your pulse is rising and you're overwhelmed. Assuming your pulse surpasses 100 beats each moment you will not have the option to hear everything that your life partner is attempting to say to you regardless of how diligently you attempt. require a twenty-minute break prior to proceeding. Remember, it's harder for a man's body to quiet down after a contention than a lady's.

Do what you really want to quiet down. For some that may be paying attention to music, taking a walk, getting what is going on before God supplication, considering something quiet and tranquil or anything helps you unwind and quiet down so you can meet up to examine your contention judiciously and securely.

❖Split the difference

Like it or not, the main answer for conjugal issues is to track down a split the difference. In a close, adoring relationship it simply doesn't work for both of you to get things generally your way, regardless of whether you're persuaded that you're correct. This approach would make such disparity and shamefulness that the marriage would endure. Before you attempt to determine a contention, recall that the foundation of any trade off is tolerating impact. This really intends that for a split the difference to work, you can't have a shut brain to your companion's perspectives and wants. You don't need to concur with all that your mate says or accepts, however you must be really open to thinking about their situation. Frequently compromise is simply a question of working out your disparities and inclinations in a deliberate manner. This is easy to do as long as you keep on following different moves toward keep your conversation from turning out to be predominantly negative.

❖Be lenient toward one another's deficiencies

Tragically, relationships again and again get impeded in "if onlies". If by some stroke of good luck your life partner were taller, more extravagant, more astute, neater, or hotter, every one of your concerns would disappear. However long this demeanor wins, clashes will be truly challenging to determine. Until you acknowledge your accomplice's blemishes and flaws, you can not think twice about. All things considered, you will be on a determined mission to modify your mate. Compromise isn't around one individual transforming, it's tied in with arranging, figuring out something worth agreeing on and ways that you can accomodate one another. This is where we can stretch out beauty to one another in our relationships.

Chapter 7

Conquer gridlock

Gridlock happens when diligent conflicts cause struggle. For instance, you're gridlocked with your companion when continuous issues lead to an absence of useful discussion. Maybe you both really can't settle on a truce. Beating gridlock isn't tied in with taking care of the issue however having a sound discussion about the circumstance. Above all, you need to grasp what's causing the issue.

To beat gridlock, here are a few stages you can take:

- Attempt to figure out the base of the issue
- Impart smoothly
- Figure out how to evaluate your nonnegotiable and adaptable region of the contention
- End the conversation on a quiet note, communicating thanks and appreciation for your accomplice

Research recommends that cheerful couples who stay together can move from gridlock to exchange about their ceaseless issues. This happens when you acknowledge your accomplice and grasp their oblivious dreams or plans.

❖Moving from gridlock to discourse

Do you feel horrendously stuck over an issue that you and your life partner just mightn't? Assuming this is the case, figuring out how to adapt to the contention might appear to be unimaginable, and you could fear your relationship is ill-fated. Be that as it may, don't surrender. Many couples figure out how to manage their gridlocked issues and construct blissful, effective connections.

A vital aspect for managing a gridlocked issue is to recall that you don't need to tackle the issue. It may very well never disappear totally. You want to move "from gridlock to exchange." Couples need to "declaw" a gridlocked issue to remove the aggravation from the issue so you can discuss it without harming one another. When you're ready to do that, you can figure out how to live with practically any interminable issue.

❖Expectations and Dreams: The Root Cause of Gridlocked Problems

The most vital phase in conquering gridlock is to find the main driver of your contention. For the most part, gridlocked clashes are an indication that either of you have profound dreams that aren't being regarded or understood. Dreams are "the expectations, yearnings, and wishes that are essential for your character and provide motivation and significance to your life." Dreams can be commonsense or significant, or a mix of both. For instance, hidden the functional fantasy about possessing a home might be the significant dream of individual freedom. Blissful couples understand it's essential to help and join each other's fantasies. Neither one of the accomplices ought normal to cover dreams or demand that the other surrender his or hers. All things being equal, the two of them share their longings and objectives, then, at that point, figure out together how to satisfy them. The test comes when dreams struggle with each other: She believes that their kids should grow up close to her family, however he needs to work for a global firm and travel the world. She needs to go to a costly school, yet he needs to stop his lucrative administration work and open an eatery.

❖Exchange: The Key to Unlocking Gridlock

Here are moves toward assist you with defeating gridlock:

- Together, pick a gridlocked issue to deal with.
- Independently record a clarification of your situation. Compose how you feel and what you need and need.
- Expound on the secret dreams that underlie your situation. For what reason is this issue so critical to you?
- Presently it is the right time to converse with discourse with each other. Every one of you ought to discuss what you've composed.
- At the point when it's your chance to tune in, don't interfere, don't pass judgment, and don't contemplate how to disprove your life partner's situation.
- Express getting it and backing of your accomplice's fantasy, regardless of whether you share it or accept it tends to be understood.

Now that you each figure out the meaning of the issue to the next individual, is there something you can do to actually manage it more? How could you both change your way of behaving to advance the circumstance, be adaptable? How might you show support for your mate's fantasy, despite the fact that it is not the same as your own? If conceivable, concoct a trade off that you can test and change depending on the situation.

Chapter 8

Make shared importance

Culture isn't restricted to nations or countries. Indeed, even two individuals who share a coexistence can make their own way of life. They can have customs, customs, stories, and convictions that tight spot them and give importance to their coexistence. "Marriage isn't just about bringing up kids, dividing tasks, and having intercourse. It can likewise have an otherworldly aspect that has to do with making an inward coexistence, a culture rich with images and ceremonies, and an appreciation for your jobs and objectives that interface you, that lead you to comprehend being a piece of the family you have become."

Shared importance doesn't mean couples concur in exactly the same words on a way of thinking of life. It implies they figure out how to work their lives. They foster a culture that consolidates both of their fantasies and objectives and that assists them with becoming together. They discuss their convictions and quest for shared belief on basic qualities. A few relationships last and function admirably without a profound feeling of shared importance. Yet, the more common importance you make, the more extravagant, really fulfilling, and more charming your relationship will be. Making shared importance includes melding your objectives, jobs, and ceremonies. You can track down satisfaction in sharing reason by permitting yourself and your accomplice to have their necessities, needs, and dreams perceived. You can make significant encounters when you share and investigate a wide range of closeness. For instance, a few couples might encounter shared importance in the event that one accomplice designs their mate's optimal birthday festivity. Imparting reason to your accomplice might assist you with feeling nearer.

❖Make an Arrangement

While it never damages to be unconstrained, intending to accomplish something together can be similarly essentially as tomfoolery and invigorating as a somewhat late supper or film. It's frequently excessively simple for couples to get stuck after they have been together for some time. Rather than agreeing to the "standard, worn out, normal, worn out," have a go at making arrangements. Doing whatever it may take to start shared importance will be a seriously big deal to your accomplice. In addition, the expectation of making shared significance together will truly talk love to them.

It doesn't make any difference what you do, simply plan something else. A couple of ideas:

- Attempt the new eatery around.
- Sleep time stories for kids, supplicating together, or paying attention to music.
- Plan a bicycle ride on a Saturday morning.
- Plan a comfortable stroll along the riverbank after work.

Keep in mind, since getting to know each other is normal when individuals have been together some time doesn't mean you can't likewise be deliberate about how you invest that energy. For example, switch off the radio and converse with each other. Ask how your accomplice's life is going and what is worrying them at this moment. You can transform pretty much any movement into an opportunity to make a common importance in the event that you are imaginative.

www.ingramcontent.com/pod-product-compliance
Lightning Source LLC
LaVergne TN
LVHW082301150826
845677LV00009B/1693

9798846087590